Body Shaming

An Unconventional Guide to Manage Yourself and Reach Your Goals Without Feeling Alone

by Hanna May Carter

Table of Contents

Introduction

"Do they even make clothes your size? How does it feel to still be shopping from the kids' section? I bet those clothes are oversized for you, too!"

"Hey! No need to visit the biology lab for a skeleton, we have one right here. I think she's even thinner than that!"

When your so-called friends make such comments about your appearance, you do not say anything. You simply laugh with them and try to make yourself feel included by being a part of their dirty jokes. You fear saying anything to them because once, you tried, and you were almost cut off from the group. *It's okay,* you tell yourself. *They are my friends, and they are just joking. They do not mean any harm and I don't want to make it seem like I'm overreacting.* But how can you help the terrible feeling? Every time such jokes are made, you go home and cry your eyes out. You look at yourself in the mirror and feel even sadder because you must live with this body. You are short and so thin that bones are visible. No clothes seem to fit nicely because your structure is so small. People might wonder, "She's thin. What is she complaining about?" but you are not thin like fashion models. You are so thin and frail that you look like you have a disease. You hate yourself because nothing seems to look good on you and everything feels horrible.

But ask yourself, *is it really my fault?* Maybe it's your genetics making your body structure the way it is. Why would you blame yourself for something like that? Moreover, the people who joke about your body and shame you for being a particular way are *not* really your friends. You are clearly sensitive about it, and either they have no idea about that, or they don't care. Either way, these people cannot be your friends because real friends do not make hurtful comments about sensitive subjects.

Body shaming is an extremely serious problem, and it is often the root cause of many mental illnesses as well. When you are shamed by your friends or family, it creates a lasting impact on your brain. You begin to see yourself through their eyes, and you feel ugly. This is the beginning of an unhealthy relationship with yourself, and it often reaches an extreme point where you hate your body and end up hurting yourself. But your body takes such good care of you. Is it correct to be so hard on it?

It is astonishing how common body shaming is. So common, in fact, that it becomes generalized. There was not much awareness about this issue amongst previous generations, which is why most people who are now in their forties or fifties do not think before calling someone "fat" or "skinny." A lot of people face body shaming from their own parents, which makes it more difficult to get over. Let's face it: most of us feel awkward about many things related to our bodies. Maybe somebody thinks that their nose is crooked, or their hair is too frizzy, or their hands are too big for their body. Most young children do not have feelings of shame or embarrassment; it is when we reach our teenage years that we become more conscious about ourselves.

The teenage years are particularly difficult because of the raging hormones and changing bodies. Puberty hits everyone differently; one person's skin can be glowing while the other person's face might suddenly be covered with acne. Self-consciousness is at its peak during this age, and if one is shamed for the way they look, it is likely that they will form negative body image issues that carry into the future. Suppose a girl has gained significant weight in her teenage years, and all her family members and friends shame her for it. She will be scarred forever, always trying to get out of that body image because it makes her feel ugly and unwanted. She might try unhealthy ways to lose weight, just so she can fit in and become pretty in everyone's eyes.

But this stops now. You must realize that you are perfect in your own way. There is no standardized measure for beauty, and you must not beat yourself up because society wants you to look a certain way. It is time to call out those people who keep telling you that you must lose or gain weight in order to become beautiful. Stop worrying about their opinions because you are awesome just the way you are. Don't be afraid to wear the t-shirt that highlights your bony frame. In fact, once you wear it, click a photo and upload it to social media because you deserve that freedom. If someone makes a comment about how the t-shirt makes you look, call them out or "unfollow" them.

You have cried in silence for a long time, but now, it is time that you start living the way you want to. In this book, I will guide you through ways to get over body shaming and to begin feeling good about yourself. I know it's not easy, especially if you have been shamed all your life, but always remember that it's never too late. Standing up for yourself should always be your priority.

Venture onto this path of self-discovery and regain your confidence because every bit of you is worth it. See yourself for who you really are. Let's learn to say no to shamers, and during this journey, learn to love yourself more.

Chapter 1:
Mirror, Mirror, on the Wall

It is your birthday next week, and you want to buy a new dress. You saw a blue one at the mall and knew that was the one you wanted to buy. When you go to the store, you find that there is only one piece available in your size. You quickly pick it up and rush to the change room before anyone else can take it. Blue is your favorite color and it always looks good on you. As you are trying the dress on, you imagine wearing it for your birthday party and how lovely you would look lovely in it. However, after you pull the zipper and look in the mirror properly, you're flooded by disappointment. The dress fits you properly, but it doesn't look good. Your arms look flabby, and the neckline highlights your improperly shaped shoulders. Why is your body like this? Why does nothing look good on you? Tears trickle from your eyes and you change back to your normal clothes. The salesperson asks whether they should pack the dress and you politely say no. You leave the store feeling disgusted about yourself because you were looking forward to buying the dress. Everything is ruined now because of how terrible your body is. You hate yourself.

If this is something you can relate to, then it is time to address some bigger issues. First things first: your body is not terrible. Often, some dresses just don't look good on us because of their design, color tone, and other similar things. If you must blame anyone, blame the dress because *you* are awesome. If you don't feel beautiful or satisfied with the way you look, then you may be suffering from body image issues.

What is Body Image?

Body image means how you see yourself and how that makes you feel. The focus is usually on height, weight, hair, shape, or size of any body part. However, the concept of body image is broader than simply what you see in the mirror. It is also impacted by your beliefs, experiences, and certain generalizations. For example, if someone has a taller and broader structure, but everyone in their family is short and small, they are likely to suffer from body image issues because it is not something that their family is used to. There may be comments from relatives like "Oh, he doesn't look like his brothers at all," which may trigger concerns about body image. Whereas somebody else with a similar body structure, whose family members are all tall and broad, might not have issues related to body image. So, it is relative. Throughout history, beauty has always been measured by popular standards. Anyone who did not fit into those standards was considered ugly. As social media creeps more and more into our modern lives, these standards are gaining permanence within our minds. Now, whenever somebody says the word beautiful, our brain immediately thinks of a tall woman, devoid of any fat on her body, with crystal-clear skin, lustrous hair, and sharp features. Whenever somebody says the word handsome, we think of a man with a body like a carved sculpture, with broad shoulders and a strong look on his face.

The Four Aspects of Body Image

Constant bombardments from the media make us feel uncomfortable about the way we look. But remember, our body image is not always bad. In fact, it may vary between positive and negative experiences, which means you can feel both good and bad about your body. On this note, let us understand the four aspects of body image:

- **Perceptual Body Image:** The way that you see your body is your perceptual body image. It will not necessarily be a correct representation of your looks.
- **Affective Body Image:** Affective body image indicates the way you feel about your body. It is usually measured by the happiness or disgust you feel when looking at yourself in the mirror.
- **Cognitive Body Image:** Your cognitive body image is the way you think about your body. This image varies from person to person and from time to time.
- **Behavioral Body Image:** If you engage in certain behaviors as a result of your body image, it is called behavioral body image. If you start adopting unhealthy eating habits in order to change the way you look, that is an example of behavioral body image.

Positive and Negative Body Image

Your body image is an aggregation of what you believe about your body, how you feel about it, and how you sense and control your body as you move. If you feel conscious while running because you feel it makes your hands look stupid, then that is an instance of a body image issue. Concerns relating to body image will range from positive (indicating satisfaction with your body) to negative (indicating dissatisfaction with your body).

Positive Body Image

When someone can respect, appreciate, and accept their body no matter what, they have a positive body image. People with a positive body image do not feel that their self-worth is associated with their physical appearance. Positive body image and body satisfaction are not the same because people might be dissatisfied with their body and still be okay with it. Having a positive body image can act as protection against developing an eating disorder. If you have a positive image, you are more likely to possess the following characteristics:

- **High self-esteem:** The way we look defines our overall respect and feelings toward ourselves. Being able to accept who we are can lead to higher self-esteem, which in turn contributes to our happiness and well-being.
- **Self-acceptance:** Once we are comfortable in our own skin, we are less likely to feel pressured by the unrealistic standards of beauty portrayed by the media. For example, if you are body positive, you will not feel sad that you don't have a tiny waist like Zendaya. You love yourself for who you are, and that helps you to appreciate yourself and others.
- **Healthy outlook toward life:** If you have a positive body image, your outlook toward many things in life will be healthy. For example, you will not feel the need to follow extreme diet or exercise routines in order to look a certain way. You will have a broader concept of beauty because you know that bodies of all shapes, sizes, and colors are beautiful.

You must remember that being body positive does not mean that you should not take care of your health or try to improve it. In fact, people who are body positive have an open outlook toward their own health. For example, when someone has a positive body image, they love and accept their body. However, they are also not scared to improve their body because they are not under any pressure to do so. Having a positive body image is important for our long-term health, but unfortunately, not many people can boast having the same.

Negative Body Image

If you have persistent negative thoughts about your appearance, then you have a negative body image. It is mostly an emotional and cognitive process, largely influenced by external factors like pressures to meet a certain appearance standard. A person suffering from a negative body image may constantly feel embarrassed and keep comparing themselves to others. They belittle themselves, as they feel inadequate and uncomfortable in their body. The following points will help you to understand whether you or someone you know has a negative body image:

- **Obsession about dieting and exercise:** If you obsess over your diet or if skipping even one day of exercise gives you anxiety, then you have a negative body image. You only eat things that will keep you in shape and never take a rest day in between your workouts because you feel you will gain weight.
- **Linking appearance with self-worth:** You feel that people will only value you if you are attractive or fit. A person with a negative body image constantly feels that there will be nothing good in life if they don't look a certain way.
- Obsession about appearance: People with a negative body image spend a lot of time talking and thinking about their appearance. They spend huge amounts of money on makeup, skincare, and clothing, and constantly check themselves out in the mirror.
- **Negative self-talk:** Shaming themselves and constantly making themselves feel inferior in

comparison to others is one of the most common behavioral patterns of a person with a negative body image. They even avoid occasions where they might feel conscious about their appearance, like swimming or social functions.

Body Image and Gender

It is a common misconception that consciousness about body image is limited to females, but studies have shown that an adolescent male is just as prone to negative body images as his female counterpart. In fact, body image issues can often be a lot worse in men due to the lack of awareness amongst them. Both men and women go through phases of negative body image issues, and both should address the same with equal importance.

Due to the rampant portrayal of unrealistic beauty standards in social media, women are constantly under pressure to look a certain way. You must have a small waist, ample hips and breasts, pouty lips, and slender thighs if you want to call yourself beautiful. How many real women have you come across who look like that? Does your mother, aunt, friend, cousin, or anyone you personally know conform to all those standards? Probably not. So, why are you beating yourself up about something that is created by the media houses to generate revenue?

Men must have muscles and abs, they must be able to lift heavy weights, and they must look like innocent little boys all at the same time. When you read these out loud, you realize how absurd all these standards are. Many young boys develop negative body image because they cannot grow a proper mustache or beard. They are teased and called "girly." The same thing happens with many young girls also, who experience growth in facial and body hair in their teens. These things happen due to the varying estrogen, progesterone, and testosterone levels in a person's body, and it is completely natural. Many women have a dense growth of body hair, and there is nothing ugly or abnormal about it. You are a human being, not a porcelain doll. You are supposed to have hair, curves, and stretch marks, and you must not be ashamed of it.

People from the LGBTQIA+ communities are at a greater risk of developing negative body images due to the discrimination they face daily. A queer person may choose to dress up or present themselves in a certain way, and if that does not conform to the general norms of society, they will be teased and harassed. Non-binary people also have a huge risk of developing negative body image issues, since their identities are different from what people are used to.

Although there is a lot of talk about body positivity and inclusivity, we are a long way from achieving it. Many celebrities publicly advocate for body positivity, so that people of all ages can seek inspiration from them. Negative body image has the potential to become life-threatening if not addressed properly. No matter your gender, age, race, or sexual orientation, you should try to eliminate the negative body image that you have created for yourself. Always remember that you are so much more than how you look.

How Does Negative Body Image Develop?

You must be aware of the popular social media trend "I Woke Up Like This," where you will find a celebrity posting a picture of themselves with this caption. Supposedly, that is how they woke up that morning. Most times, the celebrities look fresh and even glowing in the pictures, which is not something many of us can relate to. When I wake up, I look like a mess.

My hair is all over the place and my eyes are still baggy. I might be okay with that, but someone who suffers from a negative body image might easily be triggered by such posts, because they clearly do not look like that when they wake up. The celebrity might have put on makeup before posting the picture, but do we have any way to know that? No. We are led to believe that is their natural look, which is clearly different from ours. In order to replicate the look of these celebrities, many influencers and normal people also start following this trend. Maybe they are also using makeup or worse, putting filters on their pictures before posting them. But none of this would be communicated to someone who has a negative body image of themselves. Once they check a similar post, they will look at themselves in the mirror and start comparing. They will call themselves ugly, useless, and many other mean words, and for what? A post that is probably fake.

The world of social media and its pretensions contribute, to a large extent, to the development of a negative body image. Moreover, increasing pressures at the workplace often make us feel incompetent. Maybe you did not reach your monthly target, or even if you did, your colleague may have exceeded their target and received much praise from the boss. This might not have a direct relationship with your appearance, but people suffering from negative body image issues tend to relate everything with looks. The thought process can follow this pattern: *I could not even reach my target this month, but Mark did. Mark is so talented that he is bound to succeed. Look at him! He is smart, handsome, and his hair looks so good. No wonder he is so good at everything. And me? I am a pathetic loser. I cannot do my work properly and I am ugly. My hair will never be as good as Mark's and neither will anything else. I will fail at everything in life. I hate myself.*

I'm sure this has happened to you. Maybe not the exact same thing, but you must have gone through some variation of this situation and blamed yourself excessively. Body image issues can become all-pervading if you do not nip them in the bud. Whenever you experience these kinds of thoughts, try to block them. Distract yourself in any way. Watch some puppy videos or listen to calming music, but don't indulge in these thoughts. Negative body image can manifest itself in dangerous forms, so you must be careful.

Medical Conditions That Can Arise Due to Negative Body Image Issues

A negative body image causes you to look down on yourself. You demean yourself at every chance you get. This kind of behavior will cause an everlasting scar on your mind. The worse you treat yourself, the worse it gets, and you can end up experiencing far more complicated problems. If you are still thinking that it is not a big deal, that everyone feels bad about their bodies, then you must change your thoughts immediately. None of us are perfect, but that does not mean we must trash-talk ourselves. You never know when the severity of the situation will increase, leading to your illness. If you have doubts, let me explain some of the common medical conditions that can be developed if you have a negative body image:

Body Dysmorphic Disorder

With this disorder, people imagine that there are flaws in one or more parts of their bodies. These flaws are minor or non-existent, but if you have this disorder, you will always obsess over them to an extreme level. You will feel embarrassed about your appearance and ashamed of attending any social functions. In order to "fix" yourself, you seek out options like plastic surgery, or spend hours everyday grooming or checking yourself in the mirror. Cosmetic surgery might temporarily relieve you from this dissatisfaction, but in most cases, the anxiety and embarrassment return, and you are back to square one. It is a mental illness that drives you crazy, because you cannot remove your focus from that one flaw in your body, no matter how hard you try. It all starts with having a negative body image, and gradually increases each time you indulge in negative self-talk. You emphasize the flaw to a point where you become obsessed with it. Body dysmorphic disorder can lead to obsessive-compulsive disorder and many other mental illnesses.

Anorexia Nervosa

Most people who live in larger bodies tend to develop a negative body image. They become excessively conscious about their weight, which leads them to adopting unhealthy eating habits. Anorexia nervosa, or simply anorexia, is an eating disorder that leads a person to developing an intense fear of gaining weight, which is why they refuse to eat anything at all. Many people who suffer from anorexia try to control their calorie intake by vomiting after eating, misusing laxatives, or using diet aids. No matter how much weight they lose, they fear that they will gain it back, which is why they exercise excessively. Anorexia is not just about food; it is a wider mental and psychological illness that can be life-threatening and can take over your entire existence.

Bulimia Nervosa

Bulimia is another life-threatening eating disorder that can arise from a negative body image. If a person has bulimia, they will binge-eat a huge quantity of food at first, only to purge it later by vomiting. Many people try to shed extra calories by exercising excessively after eating. People suffering from bulimia self-induce vomiting, which is extremely unhealthy if done continuously. This disorder is a result of severely harsh treatment toward oneself due to self-perceived flaws. Like anorexia, bulimia is closely related to self-image and does not have much to do with food, which is what makes it so difficult to overcome.

Depression

Depression can occur due to many reasons, and a negative self-image is one of its leading causes. When you harbor negative thoughts about yourself, you are bound to feel depressed and anxious. There is a constant feeling of sadness and unfulfillment inside you, which makes everything dull and terrible. People with negative body image issues are more likely to become suicidal in the long term. Depression manifests itself in strange ways, which makes this disease so deadly. It all starts with someone passing a negative comment or unhealthy comparisons, and soon, becomes complex and difficult to treat.

A negative body image can lead to potentially dangerous disorders if not detected or treated properly. If you are suffering from a negative body image, then you must know that help is always available. If you are feeling extremely negative about your appearance, to the point that it is physically bothering you, do not hesitate to seek professional help. There is no shame in admitting that you need help, especially today, when help is abundantly available. You may be harming yourself and others around you, which is why it is important to address any issues related to depression as soon as possible.

How A Negative Body Image Leads to Body Shaming

You already know how much you can hurt yourself by developing a negative body image. Now, let's look at the other side of the story. As a child, Stella used to be chubby. Everyone thought she was cute because she looked like a teddy bear. But as she started growing up, the same people who used to call her cute and pinch her cheeks started calling her fat. Relatives no longer complimented her when she wore skirts and tunics; instead, they pointed out how her stomach was bulging, and her face wasn't fitting inside a camera frame. From this humiliation, Stella developed an extremely unhealthy image of her body, and as she reached her mid-teens, she started to diet and exercise excessively. Within a few weeks, she had lost all the extra weight and her body became the way she wanted it to be. However, even though she lost weight, her negative body image was still present. She checked herself in the mirror numerous times a day to make sure she wasn't looking fat. Her eating habits had become unhealthy, as she had cut carbs from her diet and exercised too much.

Along with all these things, Stella developed a new habit. Because she had faced much criticism and meanness due to her weight, she began directing the same attitude toward larger people. Whenever she saw someone living in a larger body, she would shame them and say mean words to them. Unbelievable, isn't it? Stella, of all people, should know how it feels when somebody shames a person for being heavy. Why would Stella do that to other people? You see, a negative body image can lead people to do all sorts of things. Because Stella had worked hard to remove that "fat" tag, she made sure to express her hatred toward anyone who is heavy. It doesn't make much sense, but it is awfully common. People with a negative body image always end up shaming others, which continues a loop.

Chapter 2:
Body-Shaming: Causes and Effects

According to a study conducted by the National Eating Disorders Association, 94% of teenage American girls—before going to college or even driving a car—have been body shamed. Not only adolescents, but also adults and elderly people have experienced body shaming. Remember Princess Leia from the *Star Wars* movies? In one of the early franchise movies, Carrie Fisher, who was then 21 years old, wore the iconic gold bikini and won millions of hearts. She was idolized by men and women alike because of her beauty. Fast forward to almost forty years later, when Carrie again appeared as Princess Leia in the latest franchise movie. Social media spewed hurtful comments about her appearance and how she looked "old." Four decades is a long time and a lot has changed since then. No one can look the same for this amount of time, no matter how much they exercise or diet rigorously. A 21-year-old and a 60-year-old are not supposed to look alike, and anyone who has a similar expectation is plain stupid. However, it's not just women who are shamed for their appearances. A picture of the famous movie star Vin Diesel recently surfaced, and he's sporting a "dad body." He was thoroughly made fun of because of how his physique had changed. Body shaming is so common that most people don't even realize they are doing it.

What Is Body Shaming?

As defined by Oxford English Dictionary, body shaming is "the act or practice of humiliating a person based on their body type by making critical and/or mocking statements about their body shape and size." Basically, it means criticizing someone because of their body type. It can range from making fun of someone casually to extremely harsh and critical remarks about their appearance. It is a form of bullying where the target is your physical appearance.

Most people do not realize they are being body-shamed, so it is important to understand what it constitutes. If someone is criticizing you based on your weight, body parts, clothes size, style, choice of clothes, hairstyle, or even the amount of makeup you are wearing, you are being body shamed. Body shaming goes way beyond the common comments like "too fat" or "too skinny." Suppose you have a lean and slender frame, and you exercise because you like to stay fit. It's likely that many of your friends or relatives have told you that you do not need to work out, since you already have a nice physique. Now, imagine that a friend posts a picture on social media for your birthday with the caption, "Happy Birthday! Have a great year and don't lose any more weight!" This might seem like a simple birthday post, but it's body shaming. Whenever anyone makes a remark about your appearance, and it's meant to be derogatory, you are being body shamed. You can be shaming yourself as well. Every time you call yourself ugly or criticize a part of your body, you are engaging in body shaming. It is important to know the ways you are shaming yourself or being shamed by others, so that you can put an end to it.

How Does Body-Shaming Manifest Itself?

As I said, you must understand the various ways that body shaming can manifest itself, so that you can identify the same and take actions against it:

- **Criticizing your own appearance:** When you criticize yourself in comparison to someone else, it is a form of body shaming. For example, imagine you are exercising at the gym and you see a guy doing push-ups and lifting weights. He is doing everything perfectly, while you are struggling with your posture and repetitions. You start thinking to yourself, *I will never be good like him. How will I ever have the body I want if I cannot do these simple squats properly? My legs are so flabby, maybe that's why I can't complete the reps.* If you are indulging in this kind of negative self-talk, then you are body shaming yourself.

- **Criticizing someone else's appearance in front of them:** If somebody is making negative remarks about your body in front of you, then you are being body shamed. Be careful because you might also be doing it to someone. Saying things like, "Why would you want to cut your hair like that? It makes your face look so big!" or "You have gained so much weight over the summer" after meeting someone are examples of body shaming. If someone is saying these things to you, it is time to call them out.

- **Criticizing someone else's appearance without their knowledge:** It is also body shaming if you are trash-talking someone behind their back. For example, at a party, you and a bunch of your friends are talking and having fun. One of your friends leaves early, and the moment they leave, the rest of you start talking about their clothes and how they looked hideous.

Somebody even adds a comment like "I know I am not pretty, but at least I don't look like them." If you or any of your friends are engaging in this behavior, then it's time to stop because you are shaming your friend.

Why Do People Engage in Body Shaming?

Most people who actively shame people based on their appearance do so for a variety of reasons. If you are being shamed by an older family member, like a grandma or an uncle, it is probably because they are not aware of the dangers it can cause. They simply think it is not a big deal. One time, my grandma told me that if I did not start losing weight soon, I would look like one of the pigs from her childhood farm. Back in my grandma's day, anyone who was overweight would be shamed and it would not be an issue, since not many people were vocal about how mean it was.

In 1942, a certain dietary supplements company came up with an illustration where thin women were making fun of a larger woman at the beach. These were the kind of advertisements that were publicly displayed during those times, so it is obvious that people from that generation thought it was normal to make fun of fat people. However, when people from the newer generation are making fun of others for their appearance, the reason might be something deeper. Over the years, companies and brands have tried to adopt a more body-positive advertising style, focusing on how "real" people look and behave. Bullying someone and shaming them about their appearance exhibits meanness. For an educated individual, there are many ways to become aware and educate themselves on the perils of body shaming. If somebody chooses to be ignorant about these issues, then that is on them.

However, there is yet another side to it. Despite so many people, including celebrities, being vocal about body shaming and advocating for body positivity, social media is still filled with people who try to look "perfect" and who shame others for not conforming to those standards.

Why Do People Put Up with Body Shaming?

The first time my grandmother called me "piggy," I was mad. I felt hurt and humiliated because she said it during Thanksgiving in front of the entire family. Just as I was about to say something, my mother held my hand tightly and gave me a look. The look meant, "Don't say anything. Keep quiet." Later, I asked her why she stopped me from confronting grandma because she was clearly wrong. My mom said that, because my grandma was old, she did not understand that it hurt me. She belonged to a different generation and she was too old to be corrected, and that is why I should keep quiet.

I am not alone. Most times, parents tell their children to keep quiet whenever a relative is saying something problematic. Grown-ups often feel bad, but they get over it because they can rationalize the entire thing. Children and teenagers, however, are more sensitive, and mean comments can significantly hurt their self-esteem. Most people put up with body-shaming because they do not want to isolate themselves from their friends or family. Confrontation often leads to an exchange of bitterness, and people want to avoid that at all costs.

Many teens put up with body-shaming to stay friends with a certain person. Even if they are being criticized, they are afraid to stand up for themselves because they might lose their position in the group. Once you start putting up with it, it gets more and more difficult to say anything, and eventually, you let people shame you all the time. Always remember that if they are shaming you, they are not your friend. Real friends support each other. They can point out your mistakes, but they will never shame you over things you don't have any control over.

Negative Impacts of Body Shaming

Let's face it: most of us are embarrassed by our bodies. Even people who are apparently perfect manage to find flaws in themselves. Moreover, various kinds of insecurities have filled our lives today. After the outbreak of the Covid-19 pandemic, many people across the world suffered pay cuts and job losses. The entire world is living with social, medical, and financial insecurities right now. The last thing we want is people shaming us about our looks. Body shaming has always been present in society, and here are some of the negative things that we may feel when it happens to us:

- **Embarrassment:** Whenever you are body shamed in public or in front of other people you know, you feel insulted and embarrassed, which is normal. If somebody calls you fat or tells you that your dress does not look good, you are filled with a sense of embarrassment and you just want to leave. It happens when you are body shaming yourself as well. If you tell yourself that you are ugly or not good enough, you start believing in it, which leads to you feeling embarrassed to face others.
- **Anxiety:** Feelings of embarrassment and shame often give rise to anxiety and panic attacks. As I said, everyone can find faults in their body, and body shaming reinstates those feelings inside our minds. Due to this feeling of imperfection, we begin to dread social functions and a sense of uneasiness creeps inside

us. As the day of socialization comes closer, this fear and restlessness increases due to the potential of criticism.

- **Sadness:** The biggest result of body shaming is that it makes us sad. There are thousands of people who have cried in silence after being body shamed. You arrive at a party that you were excited about, and the first thing your friends tell you is how bad you look. Your shoes are pathetic, and they make your feet look like claws. All the excitement and happiness you were feeling about the party vanishes, and you are filled with a sense of despair. Sadness is a common after-effect of body shaming, no matter who does it.

- **Fear:** Body shaming makes us fear social gatherings. In some extreme cases, people are even scared to look at their reflections in the mirror because they might end up disappointing themselves and others. I had a cousin with a slender build. He was shamed so much for being thin and frail that he stopped visiting anywhere or even buying new clothes, for fear that it would not fit him properly.

All these feelings can create deeper issues in someone's mind and body. In fact, fear is the greatest contributing factor to anxiety. People suffering from anxiety may experience constant sweating, restlessness, rapid heartbeat, stomach pains, diarrhea, and other uncomfortable issues.

People who have been shamed from early in their lives tend to develop extremely unhealthy coping mechanisms. Many young people who are body shamed shut themselves up completely and have difficulty expressing their feelings. Many of them cry in their room or bathroom, and then come out as if nothing has happened because they do not want others to see they feel bad. Suffering in silence is one of the most dangerous by-products of body shaming, and it can shape the entire character of a young person. If you make it a habit to stay silent, even after being insulted for no reason, you will never be able to speak up. People of all ages are subject to such insults, and even elderly people are body shamed because of their inabilities and lack of agility.

Impacts of Body-Shaming on Young People

Young people today are obsessed with social media. The life they pretend to have on the internet is more important than their real one, which is why they want to portray it as perfect. People click pictures of their food before eating it, post change room selfies, and ask other people to vote about how they look. It is nobody's fault, but the younger generation constantly validates everything in their life based on other people's opinions. Before getting a haircut, a young person may put a poll on their social media account, asking their friends and followers, "Should I get bangs?" and waiting for the response before deciding. There will be yes or no answers, but a few people will take it to the next level by saying, "You'd look pathetic in bangs because your face is huge!" or "You'd look bald if you got bangs!" This is when your insecurity will start to fuel up. You will question your decision and, as more and more mean comments start flooding in, your self-esteem will continue to plummet. Young people, especially children and adolescents, are fragile. Even the seemingly little things can have a huge and long-lasting impact on their minds. Children who experience body shaming are more likely to feel scared and insecure in life. They can grow up to be mean teenagers who either shut themselves off from the world or shame others to express their own insecurities.

Celebrities often post about their skincare regimen, diets, exercise schedules, and lifestyles. It is their job to stay connected with their fans and they do it mainly through social media. While adults understand that a movie star's diet cannot be the same as theirs, teenagers try to follow these trends in order to look cool. When they cannot do so, they are shamed. Young people are most susceptible to the negative effects of body shaming because they are still developing, physically and mentally. Changing hormone levels in their bodies can cause a lot of weird things to happen. Parents and teachers have a responsibility to teach them and make them understand that changing bodies are okay. A simple sex-education class in school is not enough to reassure them about and help them get over their insecurities. A girl who has more facial hair than some of the guys in her class is not "turning into a man." It is simply her hormones. Young boys should be educated about issues like menstruation, so that they do not shame girls for missing physical education classes once a month. This is how stigmas grow and insecurities become a part of teenagers' lives. If a boy is interested in art or cooking, they should be encouraged and not made fun of. Telling a young boy that he has soft hands like a woman is also body-shaming, not because women's hands are bad, but because the shamer is making it seem bad to them. Many young boys try to exercise or even hurt themselves, so that the scars make them look more "manly." Body shaming can have dangerous results, which is why parents should always be aware of any such issues cropping up in their children's lives.

Body Shaming of the Elderly

If you think that body-shaming is only for young people, then you are mistaken. Many elderly people are victims of body shaming as well. As one gets older, insecurities begin to change. A 70-year-old man might not be bothered about how handsome he looks, but his slow movement and inability to do regular things by himself might cause him embarrassment. Aged people often suffer from poor eyesight, which affects their ability to drive and therefore their independence. They might need assistance for walking. like a wheelchair or walker, which increases their insecurities. With age, people develop wrinkles, lose hair and teeth, and experience a weakening body. Someone who used to walk five miles every day might now struggle to go down a flight of stairs.

You might say that these things are normal and that our bodies change as we age; however, not many people can adjust to these changes easily. People like to think of themselves as strong and agile, and when they face difficulty in completing simple daily tasks, they feel sad and insecure. Many elderly people are body shamed by their children, grandchildren, or strangers because of these age-related difficulties. It is cruel, but it is common. Often, you will find children making fun of their grandparents' hanging skin or missing teeth. People get annoyed that their parents are unable to walk fast alongside them or that they ask for help at the bathroom. Shaming elderly people over their appearance and physical difficulties is insensitive because they are helpless in this regard. We should try to help them and empathize with them instead of shaming them for their difficulties.

Impact of Body-Shaming on Mental Health

Body shaming takes a huge toll on our mental health because in most cases, it takes a long time for people to realize the intensity of what is happening to them. If you are constantly shamed for having thick legs, you will feel ashamed to wear shorts or dresses that display your legs. This self-consciousness and awkwardness can often take extreme forms, which leads to people taking extreme measures to hide their flaws.

The biggest mental illness that people develop due to body shaming is social anxiety. Body shaming is usually done by friends and relatives. Once a person has been shamed by someone close, they begin to believe whatever the other person has said about them and start shaming themselves. This sense of shame and embarrassment reaches such heights that they begin avoiding social gatherings altogether for fear of being shamed again. It is one thing to call yourself ugly in front of the mirror, but when someone else does it in front of many people, it becomes unbearable. Staying home and not facing anyone is an easier option than getting insulted.

It's time to break this chain and start speaking up for yourself when things like this happen. You are already aware of the physical and mental toll that body shaming can take on you, which is why you should stop putting up with it.

I have been body shamed many times in my life and, initially, I got upset about it. I have a big family, and there was always a wedding or family function happening with many people attending, each with an opinion about how I should look. Whenever my grandmother called me "piggy" or an uncle would ask me to lose weight so that my "true beauty could reveal itself," I felt sad and often cried about it. One day, my mother caught me crying, and when I told her that I was called fat by a relative, she consoled me by saying that since they are my relatives, they say such things out of concern. When I was a child, this convinced me to a certain extent, but as I grew up, I realized that concern was no reason to shame someone. You can be concerned about your relatives and express it in a different way. Calling someone "piggy" or ugly because of their body does not exhibit care or concern; it simply shows that you are mean. Anyone who loves you will not say anything that will hurt you so deeply. Different people express things differently, and while free speech is important everywhere, make sure to express your dislike toward such comments about your body.

Your mental health is more important than those relatives showing their concern one day every year. Staying silent during these attacks only makes you more vulnerable to them, and they will keep going on. The comments will become meaner and more hurtful. Another adverse effect of body shaming is that people desperately try to change themselves based on other people's opinions. I am no exception. When I was a teenager, after one such party where I was shamed excessively, I decided to start working out and following a strict diet. I had taken a pledge to lose weight no matter what, and I was successful. For once in my life, I was looking forward to a party, so that I could hear some praise from my relatives. But guess what happened? They started telling me that, since I'd now lost weight, I could start focusing on my skin and hair because they needed so much work. The imperfections in my skin were highlighted once my weight was reduced. That day, I realized that no matter what you do, body shamers will not stop because they don't care about your health; they simply want to bring you down. Staying true to yourself is the best thing that you can do because your body is beautiful. Learning to silence your shamers is important for your physical and mental well-being.

Chapter 3:
Shame on You, Shamers

Dave is a 27-year-old lawyer. He works for a big law firm in New York, and he is quite successful. Apart from his work, he likes to play the guitar, watch foreign movies, and eat good food. He has a big friend circle, and he meets with them every other weekend. They usually visit a nice restaurant and then hit their favorite pub for some drinks afterward. Dave has a pretty good life, and he enjoys it most of the time, except when he sees his friend Emily. Emily tends to make fun of others and humiliate them for their appearance. Most people who are friends with Emily know about it, and they don't tell her anything because she is a good person otherwise. She helps people and would be there if you need someone to talk to. But every conversation you have with her is accompanied by a friendly jab. Later, she will hug the person she insulted and say, "I was only kidding dude!" and then act like everything is normal.

But Dave did not like her. They were all a part of the same group since high school, and beginning in their teens, she made insulting comments about Dave's hair, which is thin with a receding hairline that started when he was around sixteen or seventeen years old. Boys that age usually don't suffer from hair loss, and Dave's parents consulted doctors too. The doctors said there was nothing wrong with him medically, that his hair was simply thin, and that he would lose most of his hair quickly. Dave tried many hair products, but nothing worked. His teens were spent with many insecurities, and people like Emily only made it worse. Even today, whenever he met her, she never left an opportunity to make fun of his receding hairline, and every time she said something about his hair, Dave still felt embarrassed and ashamed of his appearance.

He had made his peace with his body and was finally beginning to accept himself for who he was, but each time he met Emily, it felt like he was back to square one. However, he never had the nerve to say anything to her because she was always a popular person and people liked being around her. Picking a fight with her could mean alienation from the entire group and moreover, Dave did not like confrontations of any kind.

Today is the date for one of their bi-weekly meetups. Dave has reached the restaurant, along with most of his friends. Emily had let them know she was busy that weekend, and that she would try to join them for drinks later. It was a relief for Dave, and he was having a lovely evening...until the moment Emily stepped into the pub. The first thing she said was, "Woah Dave! Now you officially have less hair than my grandpa. Let me see your head so that I can count the hairs on it!"

Dave usually stays silent when she says these kinds of things, but today, something snapped inside him, and he decided he has had enough. "That's not cool, Emily. You know I have had problems with my hair since my school days. Why do you keep making fun of it?" Emily was quite startled and said, "I was just kidding Dave. You know I don't mean to hurt you." Dave replied, "But you do, and you've been doing that for years. I was not brave enough to stand up for myself, but I don't think I am going to put up with this body-shaming anymore." Dave had thought his reaction would be perceived as overdramatic, but one of their other friends agreed with him and said, "He's right, Emily. You make fun of my acne, even though I've not had it for years. It's not cool." The atmosphere at the pub had certainly changed, and Emily left after one drink. It might have been awkward, but it was necessary.

Body shaming is terrible and the person who goes through it can feel a lot of distress. Dave had the option of staying silent, but he did the right thing by calling her out in front of everyone because that taught her a lesson. No matter how hard it is, sometimes you must stand up to your shamer. Your body deserves that justice.

Stand Up to Your Shamer

Body shaming is not always direct comments about your weight or hair. Many indirect comments from your loved ones are also considered shaming. Things like, "You are tall for a girl," or, "Your body is weak for a guy" are also forms of body shaming because the other person is making a remark about your body and comparing you to general standards. Relatives telling you whether you should eat that piece of cake is also body shaming. You can be shamed by your partner as well if they are making remarks about the way you dress or your looks. When a partner tries to dress you up in a certain way, you should make sure that they are not doing so to change your appearance. If they like a piece of clothing and think it would look good on you, go ahead and buy it. But asking you to change your hair color or drastically alter the way you dress can indicate that they are trying to make changes in your looks because they do not approve of your style.

How to Spot Signs of Body Shaming?

Understanding that you are being shamed is the first step to standing up to your shamer. Every person is different, and they are triggered by different things. For your clarity, these are a few things that you should look out for if you feel you are being shamed:

- **Talking about their own weight:** All of us know at least one person who loves talking about their own weight. This includes details about how much they weigh, how much they used to weigh five years ago, and what they are doing to maintain their weight. If you are on the heavier or lighter side of the scale, it is bound to make you uncomfortable because your weight is not a topic that you openly discuss. Remember that body shaming is not always direct; your feelings are the most important thing, and if you feel that you are being shamed, then you are.

- **Unwanted advice on diet and exercise:** There is probably a fitness freak in your social circle who goes on and on about their workout regimen and that new diet they are following. If hearing about diet and exercise triggers you, then it is body shaming. Maybe you joined the gym but could not continue due to other commitments, and now, every time you hear about the gym or drive past one, you are reminded of your failure. It does not always have to make sense to others if it is making sense to you.

- **Comments about food:** Suppose you are out with your friends and someone says they will not be eating pizza because of the carbohydrate overload, or they will skip dessert so that they can stay in shape. These comments could make you feel bad about yourself because you were on your second slice of pizza and had eaten two candy bars for breakfast. Comments about food choices often invoke feelings of shame, especially when you like eating that food or are not putting any effort into eliminating it, despite knowing the side effects.

- **Equating beauty with body size:** This one is direct. If anyone says that being thin or muscular is the only way to become attractive, then they are body shaming all people who do not fit the bill. Every person is unique and beautiful in their own way, and their body shape has nothing to do with it. Hearing about how women find men with a good body attractive can trigger feelings of embarrassment because not everyone has the body of a movie star. Whenever someone equates body shape with beauty, it causes distress to everyone who considers themselves otherwise.

- **Wardrobe and styling choices:** Older people who dress more conservatively tend to have opinions about how the younger generation should dress. My grandmother almost had a heart attack when she saw my cousin with blue hair. Many people like to comment on other's dressing sense. It's not always even negative; comments like, "Why don't you wear more blue? It will bring out your eye color!" are also forms of body shaming because they are indirectly criticizing your looks and indicating that your current dressing sense does not showcase your features.

- **Inquiring if they lost weight:** Often, when somebody asks if you have lost weight, you take it as a compliment; however, is it really praise or is it an indirect indication that you used to be fat? When people tell you that you are looking good because you lost the extra pounds, it is a form of fat-shaming. Losing weight is good for our overall health but telling someone they look good *because* they have lost weight is body shaming.

Often, people do not even realize they are shaming others because many of these comments are made unconsciously. Therefore, it's important to educate yourself, so that you don't do or say anything that might hurt someone you love. We are all vulnerable, and it is best to educate yourself about matters so that you can avoid uncomfortable situations.

Responding to Body Shaming

It is not essential that you respond to body shaming, but you must do it if you feel that it is causing you distress.

The first thing that you should always try to do is call out the people who are body shaming. Even if you see that someone is being shamed, try to stand up for them because turning a blind eye to these things normalizes them. If you can stop somebody from shaming others, you must do it. Once you start standing up for others, a part of you starts to believe that body shaming is wrong. It also gives you strength to stand up for yourself and call out your own shamers. The next time that somebody is gossiping about somebody's weight, don't participate in the discussion and ask them to stop. It must start somewhere.

If you are often on the receiving end of body shaming, it might be a good idea to think of a response beforehand. It can be a sarcastic comment or something that strikes a more serious chord, but thinking of a response can be useful because, when you are being shamed, your emotions can take over your rational thought process. When somebody is shaming you deliberately, they want to ambush you. When you retort with a well-thought response, they are likely to be confused and stop. When you are thinking of an answer, it helps you to rationalize it, which makes your shamer realize that you are taking it seriously.

However, everything is relative, and if you do not feel like picking up a fight with your shamer, then don't do it. You do not have to educate everyone, and if you don't have the mental fortitude to have all such conversations, simply ignore them. Picking your battles is important when dealing with body shaming because it often takes a toll to respond and fight back. It is your life, and the main objective is to stay physically and mentally healthy. If calling someone out suits you, do that. If ignoring and blocking your shamers gives you peace, then go for it.

Some Things to Remember If You Encounter Body Shaming

Like most difficult things, standing up for yourself when you are being shamed is easier said than done. Often, people go numb when they encounter body shaming. People are caught off-guard because nobody expects to be insulted, and even if they do, it still hurts. It might not be until hours later that it hits you and you start feeling shame, embarrassment, and pain. Therefore, you must understand how to process the entire thing and to remember these few things when you are encountering body shaming:

It's Mostly About Them

Whenever we encounter body shaming, our first reaction is to feel hurt, shamed, and insulted all together. We think that the shamer is correct, and that we really are ugly or fat or skinny or whatever they are calling us. But it is important to remember that when someone is shaming you, it is *their* misconceptions and prejudices speaking. It has little to do with how you are. They might want to make you feel terrible, but you do not have to think about those words for more than a moment.

In order to deal with body shaming, you must learn not to take their words to heart because you'll feel overwhelmed coming up with any response. If someone has insulted you and you felt particularly terrible afterwards, take a moment to recover from it. Step back and take a deep breath because it always helps to calm down. Unless you are calm, your brain will not be working properly, and you will not be able to come up with any kind of response. Remember that your response does not always have to be a fight. You can simply let them know that you do not approve of such comments.

Defend Yourself and Stand Up for Others

I believe that body-shamers get away with making mean comments because *we let them* get away with it. When my grandma used to call me "piggy" at every social function, I felt bad but since I was still a child, I didn't say anything to her. My emotions always got the better of me, and I would go to the bathroom and cry. But what's more surprising is that none of my relatives ever did anything to put a stop to it. Years later, my grandma kept on saying mean things about my body, hair, and many other things, but nobody ever said anything. Body shaming has become such a big social evil because nobody ever stands up for others. Therefore, if you see that someone is being shamed and you have the mental fortitude for it, stand up to the shamer. Many people think that it is not their place to defend someone else, but you will be surprised at how many people are looking for support. Think about it: when you are being shamed and feeling totally helpless, wouldn't it be comforting if someone stood up for you?

It's Okay If You Are Not Feeling Up for It

Sometimes, we do not have the energy to stand up for anything. The insults hurt so much that we want to curl up to our bed, pull a blanket over our heads, and cry into the pillow. If you are feeling like that, you should do exactly what feels best. Pick up a tub of ice cream, too, for some extra love. You have every right to avoid all interactions in order to preserve your sanity. Moreover, not everyone can be empathetic or to understand what they are doing wrong, so it is best to let them be. If someone makes a remark about your weight during a dinner party, and you know that calling them out will lead to a series of uncomfortable moments, then let it slide. Your peace of mind is most important, and you must do everything in your power to protect it. Some people will never get it, no matter how much you try to make them understand. They might even try to pick up another fight with you, trying to explain why they said what they said, so it is best to avoid these people.

Many People Are Doing It Unconsciously

There are not many instances in real life when someone simply comes up to you and calls you "ugly" or "fat" to your face. Most forms of body shaming are subtle, and people doing it often do not realize the same. When someone tells you that a particular dress looks flattering on you, they may be just complimenting you but there is a body shaming subtext that cannot be ignored. Calling someone flattering or attractive *only* when they wear a particular dress or do their hair in a certain way implies that they do not look beautiful the rest of the time. When they start working out and developing a muscular body, many young boys hear compliments like. "Now you are looking like a man." While the person saying it simply wants to praise the boy's new look, there is an underlying aspect of body shaming that implies you need to be muscular to look like a man. If someone you know and love is saying these things, make sure to have an honest dialog with them. Let them know that these compliments do not make you happy; rather, it points out that your beauty or attractiveness is linked to a dress or your physique.

It Is Perfectly Okay to Be Angry

Society always imposes certain behavioral restrictions on us. Right from childhood, we are asked to behave properly in front of guests and never be rude to them, even if they say something objectionable. As an adult, I have learned that you are under no obligation to always be on your best behavior. If someone is shaming or insulting you, you have every right to be angry. When you feel your blood boiling after hearing shameful comments about your appearance, you can get angry. Don't let anyone convince you otherwise.

However, anger that comes to you in the heat of the moment is rarely productive. You can scream at your shamer and call them out verbally, but in order to make it more impactful, let them feel your anger rather than hear it. Remove yourself from that position and let them know that you are unapologetic about it. It often becomes difficult to behave like this with your elders but remember that you are not at fault here—they are. They have no right to speak ill about your appearance, and if they do, they must be ready to deal with the consequences.

It Might Be an Opportunity to Educate

Despite all the negativity, there are many people who are willing to learn and educate themselves about body shaming. Maybe they said something wrong without realizing that it is hurting someone. When someone like this has shamed you, you could take the opportunity to educate them and let them know why it is not okay to say what they did. Not all interactions have to be negative, and if you see that someone is open-minded, try to educate them so that they do not repeat such comments to someone else. I understand that it is not easy to educate people when you are feeling insulted, but if you can educate at least one person, the world would be a better and safer place for everyone. We all have a responsibility, and we should try to do our bit to make things better.

Not Every Experience Will Be the Same

When I was in college, there was a group of mean girls who liked to pick on people just for the fun of it. They were popular, and nobody would cross them. I faced a lot of bullying and body shaming from these girls over the four years of my college life. I was still not mentally strong enough to stand up to them, which is why I suffered in silence. One time, I got mad and picked a fight with one of them when they fat-shamed me. But things quickly took a turn for the worse, and they started shaming me for behaving like a baby. After that, I kept quiet and avoided them until the end of term.

A few years later, when I was working, there was a similar woman at the office who liked to boast about her beautiful figure and how she ate nothing but salads. One day, we were all having lunch together, and as I was about to start eating my burger and fries, she told me, "You should really eat something healthier for your lunch. It will do wonders to your skin and overall health." There it was—the same old body-shaming once again. However, by then, I was strong and had learned the trick to standing up to my bullies. In response, I said, "Hey, thanks a lot for your concern, but it's not your place to tell me what I should or should not eat. These comments trigger me, and I don't approve of them." She apologized and that was the end of it. That night after work as I was walking to my car, she caught up with me and told me something surprising. "Hi, I am so sorry for what I said during lunch. I was speaking from genuine concern and I had no idea that it was triggering for you. Thank you so much for letting me know. I would never bring up these things in front of anyone. The world is already suffering; the least I can do is be kind." We became friends after that.

The reason I shared these two stories is to make you understand that not every experience of body shaming will be the same. While some people might be simply cruel, there will also be people who are nice. You must not let one experience define everyone. Try to keep an open mind.

Standing up to your shamer and dealing with insults becomes easier if you can remember these things. However, since most of our lives have moved online, social media has also been filled with haters and body shamers. It often takes extreme forms and that is why it is important to know and educate yourself about how you can overcome cyberbullying.

Chapter 4:
Cyberbullying and Overcoming Virtual Body Shaming

Virtual communication has reached its peak because the entire world is now obsessed with it. People are glued to their phones all day, reading posts and uploading pictures about everything in their lives. The cyberworld has its perks—it has made official and personal communication significantly easier, and it gives us easy access to information from all over the world. For the older generation, social media helps keep them in touch with their long-lost friends. However, the younger generation uses social media on an extreme level, sharing memes and videos all day. The quality of content in the various social media platforms is enriching, including artists sharing their artwork and would-be reporters doing in-depth analysis of popular TV shows and fantasy stories. However, there's a darker side to this, too. People like to post personal information, like their experiences, photos, and videos, on social media. Whenever too much personal information is being shared, it exposes a person's life and vulnerabilities, which is where the bullies come into the picture.

Social media is filled with people who are constantly making hurtful comments about peoples' posts. What might start as comments like, "You could have clicked this picture from a better angle," or, "The lighting is not good," can quickly escalate to hurtful and insulting comments that could cause great distress to the person receiving them.

What Is Cyberbullying?

Cyberbullying is the bullying of people over digital platforms. It is mostly targeted toward children and adolescents, but people of any age can become victims. It can take place on social media platforms, messaging and gaming forums, and through mobile phones where people view, participate in, or share any form of content. It includes spreading lies about a certain person, posting embarrassing pictures of them, sending hurtful messages or threats, impersonating someone and sending mean messages to others on their behalf, and so on. Sometimes, cyberbullying may cross the line into unlawful or criminal behavior as well. These are the popular places in the virtual world where you can experience cyberbullying:

- Social media outlets, such as Facebook, Instagram, TikTok, Twitter, and Snapchat.
- Text messages and messaging apps on phones and tablets.
- Online chatting forums, instant messaging, and chat rooms.
- Message boards and forums like Reddit.
- Email.
- Online gaming forums.

Cyberbullying is now a rising concern, since children are getting access to mobile phones, tablets, and computers from a young age, which exposes them to a variety of people. The effects of cyberbullying can be devastating, since the person experiencing it is helpless and with no clue about how to get out of it.

Special Concerns Related to Cyberbullying

Since we are constantly active on various social media platforms, the content we share can easily be accessed by friends, family, and even strangers. For example, if you have a public profile on Instagram, anybody can easily browse your profile and take a screenshot of a silly post you made three years ago. It creates a permanent public record, which often becomes a cause for concern because schools, colleges, and prospective employers skim through the social media platforms of their applicants to determine what kind of a virtual persona they have. Every institution or company wants to make sure that they are not associating themselves with a bully. Cyberbullying is especially concerning because of its following features:

- **Persistence:** No matter how much bullying one is undergoing, they cannot live away from their phone. They might turn it off for a while, but they will open it again after a while, which creates a persisting impact on their mind. Digital devices enable you to stay online 24/7, and that is why finding respite from it can be difficult.
- **Permanence:** Unless you are deleting or reporting a post, all the information that you share on your social media platform is permanent and can be accessed by people even years later. A bad online reputation can significantly harm your prospects for college applications and job opportunities.
- **Difficult to notice:** The biggest concern of cyberbullying is that it is not easily noticed by other people. Face-to-face bullying can have many witnesses and often, your friends or even strangers may help you. However, in the case of cyberbullying, since the entire thing is happening on phones or online, nobody can see

or understand when anything wrong is going on. The person undergoing the bullying also finds it difficult to speak up, which makes it more concerning.

Often, physical bullying accompanies cyberbullying, making the impact even more strong. In such cases, people find it difficult to escape, and they are constantly living with fear and insecurities.

How to Determine Whether You Are Being Cyberbullied

A bully might brush off their behavior as a friendly jab or a harmless joke. However, it is not for them to decide, and if somebody feels that they are being bullied, then theirs is the opinion that matters. Even with cyberbullying, someone would want to claim that they were only joking and that there is nothing serious about whatever they are doing. But it is *you* who must decide if the joke has gone too far. Cyberbullying can be uncomfortable because it attracts attention from many people, including strangers. If you are having doubts about whether the "jokes" that are being played on you constitute cyberbullying, here are a few tips that will help you gain clarity on this subject:

Are You Being Excluded?

Exclusion is a common phenomenon in the case of physical bullying as well. If your friends are deliberately excluding you from group chats or ignoring your messages on posts, then it is a form of cyberbullying. Suppose one of your friends posted a picture, and you commented asking in what place the picture was taken. You even tagged them while posting the comment. There were many comments after yours, and replies were given to every comment except yours. This can be an intentional attempt to leave you out from the virtual conversation.

Are You Being Harassed?

Harassment is a broad category under which many different things can take place. If you want to understand whether you are being harassed virtually, then decide if someone is sending you threatening or harmful messages constantly with the intention of causing you harm. If the answer is yes, then you are being cyberbullied.

Has Your Personal Information Been Shared?

If someone has shared any of your personal information without your consent, that constitutes cyberbullying. Personal information can include photos, documents, or screenshots of messages from a personal chat. You had no idea and then, one morning, you open social media to find that all your messages are being circulated. You have been cyberbullied. This act of sharing personal information without one's consent is known as outing or doxing.

This can also include trickery, where someone becomes friends with you and slowly gains your trust. When you trust them and have shared personal information with them, they circulate your personal information across digital platforms. This is extremely common after a breakup, when people expose intimate pictures of their ex-partners for revenge or simply for the fun of it.

Are You Being Stalked?

Cyberstalking is an extremely serious form of cyberbullying and can include monitoring, threats of physical harm, and false accusations, and is often accompanied by offline stalking. If something like this is happening to you, then you must seek help from the police, as cyberstalking is a criminal offense.

Is Someone Using Your Account Forcefully?

Although this does not happen much with adults, it is particularly common among children. A bully might use your account to spread harmful and objectionable information from your account. This is dangerous, since people are going to perceive that you are the one sharing those disturbing posts. This is known as frapping, and it can be potentially dangerous if the bully is using your account to spread racial or homophobic slurs to ruin your reputation.

Apart from these, there may be instances where someone you know has created a fake virtual identity for the sake of cyberbullying. This is known as masquerading, and it can involve the creation of a fake email I.D., social media profile, and even pictures just to trick you. Trolling is also a form of cyberbullying, where haters spread disturbing information about someone just to ruin their reputation.

Spotting the Signs and Understanding the Effects of Cyberbullying

Understanding what constitutes cyberbullying will help you understand whether you are a victim of the same. Like all kinds of shaming and bullying, victims of cyberbullying also have a tough time identifying whether they are undergoing it.

Spot the Signs

Despite knowing the above points, you might still not be convinced that you are a victim of cyberbullying. Look out for these signs in order to understand if you or someone you know is undergoing cyberbullying:

- You feel uneasy and scared of going outside because you fear that whatever is happening online can continue in real life as well.
- You feel anxious while using social media, and you always keep your phone with you so that nobody can see the things going on.
- Every time you are done scrolling through your news feed, you feel angry and frustrated because of the repeated messages you are receiving.
- You can sense something is not right, but you never discuss anything with your family or friends.

These are some of the signs that indicate you might be a victim because you are clearly uncomfortable during your time in the virtual world.

Understand the Effects

Once you begin to spot these signs of your interactions online, try to relate them with some of the things you might be feeling. Cyberbullying can be painful because there seems to be no respite from it, not even inside your own home. It chases you and brings you down, no matter how hard you try to avoid it. These are some of the possible physical, mental, or emotional effects if you are a victim of cyberbullying:

- **Unexplained weight loss or gain:** One of the most common effects of bullying is depression, which can cause you to binge eat or refuse food altogether. This is the cause of unexplained weight loss or gain. Much of cyberbullying is about body-shaming, so these are quite common side effects.
- **Trouble sleeping:** It is a common habit for most people to check their phones first thing in the morning and right before going to bed at night. When you are being cyberbullied, it is probable that you will have trouble falling asleep or getting out of bed because of what you saw in your social media feed.
- **Loss of interest in everything:** Bullying creates a complex inside the mind of the victim, which causes them to lose interest in everything they liked. The only thing in their minds is the trauma that they are going through. This kind of behavior is extremely common among children who are experiencing cyberbullying.

Victims of cyberbullying isolate themselves from their friends and families because of the fear and insecurity of being bullied more. The feeling of judgment prevents them from speaking to anyone, and they often refuse clinical help as well. In many extreme cases, victims become suicidal. The biggest problem with cyberbullying is that most people do not realize how traumatic words on a mobile or computer screen can be. One might argue that real-life bullying is so much worse because escaping from a tormentor is not as easy as switching off your phone or computer. Unfortunately, the effects of cyberbullying are deeper, and they don't simply go away when the electronic device is switched off. Victims of cyberbullying often feel that they have no safe space to go to, which leads to more panic and anxiety.

Cyberbullying and Body-Shaming

Social media has given easy access to body shamers who are bullies. Saying something to their face might often be difficult but writing a mean comment on someone's post takes no time or courage at all. Today, most body shamers have moved online, and proof of that can be found in the comments of any celebrity. Whenever any celebrity posts a picture, a group of people leave extremely mean comments about their appearance, body shape, and how they have dressed. If beautiful celebrities are bullied so much, imagine what normal people must go through. Moreover, normal people do not have the privilege or power to shut these people down by making bold statements to the media. They must put up with the shaming for days, weeks, or months, always hoping that these people will eventually forget about them.

Posting any kind of picture on social media becomes a nightmare for people because they fear the mean comments. Body shaming on social media is an extremely common phenomenon because people can simply post insulting comments and try to bully the victim. Such shaming makes people feel embarrassed of their identity, which leads them to adopt unhealthy means of making themselves more attractive. Some people are so affected by cyberbullying that they withdraw themselves from their friends and social circle.

Standing Up to Cyberbullying

Do you know what makes bullies seem so powerful? It is not always physical, meaning that your bully does not always need to be bigger than you. Bullies are good at playing with your mind and exploiting your insecurities. In the case of cyberbullying, due to the absence of a physical bully, the effect is more aggravating. Bullies will write mean comments on your post, send you threatening messages, and can even harass you in person. While many people still do not understand why cyberbullying is such a big deal, it can destroy a person's reputation and take away their peace of mind forever. Therefore, no matter how hard it seems, you should take steps to stand up to the people engaging in cyberbullying.

Who Should You Talk to?

The first step in addressing cyberbullying is to identify it and find someone you can talk to. If you are comfortable with your own family members or friends, you can speak to them about the abuse you are facing. If you are still in school or college, you can speak to counselors or your favorite teacher. If you don't feel comfortable confiding in people you know, reach out to a professional therapist, as they can guide you about the future course of action.

In case you are being bullied on a social media platform, there are ways to restrict your account, including unfollowing or blocking. All popular platforms, like Facebook, Instagram, and Twitter, have a forum where one can report cyberbullying. The platforms take these complaints seriously. They are obligated to keep their users safe from any kind of abuse, so your problems will be addressed.

Do It Even If It Feels Uncomfortable

Standing up to your bully, whether physically or online, takes a lot of courage and it is okay if you are feeling uncomfortable or scared while doing so. Fear is the biggest driving factor behind silence. Shaming has made the victim more insecure, and they simply don't have the guts to face their abuser. Try to overcome the fear by talking to someone, and act only when you feel you are ready. Cyberbullying can become a criminal offense if it crosses a certain boundary. Try to learn about the laws and regulations in your state related to cyberbullying. When you are equipped with the relevant information, it makes you feel more confident about taking the next step.

Is It Possible to Fight Cyberbullying Without Giving Up Access to the Internet?

I remember that when my twelve-year-old niece first told her parents about being cyberbullied, their first reaction was, "Close all your social media accounts. Don't even go near your phone or laptop." She was a good kid, so she listened to them. However, in today's generation, do you think this is feasible advice to give to a child? When the Covid-19 pandemic broke, all schools started conducting online classes. During these times, if you tell a child to stay away from phones or computers, you are asking them to give up their education. Instead of prohibiting them, I think, as parents, you must address the issue and educate yourself about the ways you can overcome cyberbullying without sacrificing anything. Facebook and Instagram have algorithms that automatically hide and filter comments that can be triggering or upsetting to people. You can simply enable that option in your profile. You also have the option of reporting a post or even an advertisement if you feel it constitutes cyberbullying.

If a child has experienced cyberbullying, you must let them know that it is not their fault. Restricting the use of electronic devices may lead them to believe that they have done something wrong, and now, they must hide in order to eliminate that mistake. This can cause a life-long fear of self-expression and permanent damage to self-esteem.

Some Tips for Standing Up to Cyberbullying

Whether it is happening to you or someone you know, you must always stand up to cyberbullying because it is wrong, and nobody should have to go through it. Talking to a trusted person and gathering information about your rights will help you move in the right direction. These are some tips that will help you stand up to cyberbullying:

- Firstly, if your bully is part of the same institution that you are in, make sure to report them to the authorities. Most of the time, cyberbullying is done by someone we know, like someone from our school, college, or workplace. Taking the matter to the concerned authority will always yield useful results, since any kind of institution has rules and procedures to be followed for cyberbullying. That is probably the best thing you can do to them for whatever they have done to you.

- Secondly, whenever you are about to report a case of cyberbullying, make sure that you have collected enough evidence to support your complaint. This is a lot like a legal case, and since it is a serious accusation, the authorities will need conclusive evidence. Take screenshots of all the comments and private messages that you feel constitute bullying. Gather the information and organize them chronologically, so that the authorities can understand how it began and escalated. If you are the one undergoing the bullying, it might be difficult to do so because of the emotional toll it takes, which is why it is important that you have someone trusted to help you out.

- Thirdly, take care of yourself during this entire process. Calling out a bully and acting against them might seem cathartic, but it is extremely draining. When you are reporting your bully to the concerned authorities, you must narrate the incidents again and again, which takes a toll on our mental health. Whenever something like this happens, the only thing we want is to forget about it. Talking about it constantly is bound to trigger your insecurities, which is why you must take care of your physical and mental well-being.

- Finally, surround yourself with people who care. Bullying often makes us want to close all doors and lock ourselves inside our pool of misery, but isolation makes these things worse. Even if you are a reserved person in general, open up to the people you are close to and talk to them about the abuse. It is going to be very difficult but try to do it slowly. You can seek help from a therapist as well, and they will guide you about how to open up to people without feeling overwhelmed. When you learn to talk to trusted people about the bullying, you will be able to process what happened in a better way. You might even start to feel comfortable talking about it, and that will make things easier.

A lot of people believe in retaliation as a means of standing up to their cyberbully. When you get back to the bully with more hurtful comments and messages, there is little chance that they will take a lesson from it and stop. They feed off this attention and will get back to you with more insults. Therefore, it is extremely important to choose your actions wisely; otherwise, it will simply add to your distress.

The sole reason why bullies make mean comments is because they want you to feel bad about yourself. It is not ignorance or an honest mistake, but plain cruelty. A couple of years back, an old friend of mine from school sent me a friend request on Facebook. I added him because we went to middle school together and used to be friends. I never got around to sending him a message because it felt awkward after so many years. I didn't notice until a few days later that this guy had started reacting "Haha" to all my posts. No matter what I posted, he reacted with the funny face emoji, as if whatever I was posting was hilarious, including all the pictures, posts, or anything I shared.

I did not pay much attention to it until one day, I saw that he had reacted "Haha" to a post where I was reminiscing about my long-deceased aunt, who I greatly admired. That was when I lost it and decided to send him a message, asking why he kept reacting with the funny face emoji to all my posts. That is when the bullying started. It was as if he was waiting for my message all along. He started throwing insults at me, criticizing my lifestyle, my looks, and everything else he could think of. It seemed that he had planned to do this for a long time, and that he had thought carefully about what he was going to say. I felt helpless because he was cyberbullying, but it was not something that I could report. I couldn't call the police and tell them that a person was reacting with the funny face emoji to all my posts because it did not seem like a justified complaint.

It was getting unbearable, the insults were subtle and not too intense, but it was getting to me. This was troubling me, and that is when I decided to bring it up with my therapist. She reassured me that I was not overreacting, and that the best thing I could do to silence this bully was to ignore him. I never thought that this could work, but it did. I stopped reading his messages and deleted him before even opening the chat. I deleted every comment he wrote on my posts and ignored the "Haha" reactions. It took a while, but eventually, he disappeared from my life.

When you are being cyberbullied or body shamed online, it is your mind that is affected the most. You cannot function properly unless your mind is working correctly. Therefore, you must try to take care of your mental health because the road to self-acceptance is an uphill one. Winning over the fear and shame that surrounds your body is the healthiest coping mechanism that you can adopt and for that, you must nurture your mind so that self-love becomes organic.

Chapter 5:
Mind Matters Over Everything

Cyberbullying, body-shaming, and all kinds of insults can have a deep impact on our minds. It can make us feel defeated, scared, and angry. A person who encounters body-shaming on a regular basis tends to withdraw themself from the entire world because they cannot bear the emotional pain anymore. It is perfectly normal to feel this way, and you shouldn't let anyone convince you that you are overreacting. Your feelings matter, which is why you should start taking care of your mental health so that you can cope with the effects of body-shaming in a healthy way. When you have been attacked by your shamers, you might feel that you have hit rock bottom and there is no escape from this terrible nightmare, but help is always available if you want to seek it. If you do not do something to get through the agonies associated with body shaming, then it will define your entire life.

We often feel that taking care of ourselves means watching a good movie, going on a self-date, or having a spa day. But mental health is so much more than just these things. It is an all-encompassing process that changes your outlook by changing your daily routine, food habits, and sleep patterns. People who have undergone body shaming in their lives have suffered extensive unkindness toward their bodies. This kind of behavior leaves a scar on our mental as well as emotional health.

Why Body-Shaming Is More About Your Mind Than Your Body

Sally is a middle-aged woman. She is calm and quiet and wears the same kinds of clothes to work every day. Her friends and colleagues often ask her to go out with them, but she always politely declines. It seems like her life is always on the same track, and she never does anything out of the ordinary. She looks like someone who is never truly happy, and there's always a sad vibe about her. She never behaved rudely to anyone, but it's obvious that she's not interested in anything. Although there is nothing wrong with being this way, let's delve deeper into why Sally behaves this way.

If we went back around twenty years in Sally's life, we would find a lively teenage girl. She loved bright colors and couldn't stop talking. Every other day, she would paint her nails with a shocking neon color. One summer, just before the holidays were about to end, she went to a salon for a haircut. Sally was in an experimental phase in her life then and wanted to try out something new. The popular TV show *Friends* had just aired, and everyone was going crazy for the characters and their styles. Sally always thought she was like Jennifer Aniston's character, Rachel, which is why she decided to style her hair like that. It was a popular haircut in those days and when the haircut was done, Sally couldn't control her excitement. It was as if she had become a part of the show!

However, life had other plans for Sally. The moment she stepped into her house, her dad criticized her haircut, telling her that she looked "cheap." Sally was disheartened, but she did not pay much attention to her father, since she knew he was a bit old-fashioned. But that was just the beginning. The next week when she went back to school, all her classmates started making fun of her. "Do you think cutting your hair like that is going to make you look like Rachel?" "Too bad the salon didn't change your face." These were some of the many "friendly jabs" she heard throughout the next term. By the time the Christmas holidays came, Sally was so fed up that she cut her hair short, so that the impact of the previous haircut was significantly reduced. But that was not the end of it. Those insults scarred Sally much more than anyone else could have imagined. She became quiet and stopped painting her nails. The bright clothes slowly started turning into pastels, and soon, all her ideas about experimenting were gone. Those few months of body shaming had turned her into a completely different person. Her hair soon grew back to the way it was before the haircuts, but her confidence never did.

Since problems of the mind are not always visible, people tend to ignore them. If there was a wound on your leg, would you see the doctor for it? Of course! Then why would you ignore your wounded mind? The biggest problem with body-shaming is that once you encounter it, you develop a kind of hatred toward yourself and your body. The words of your shamer get inside your head and you start to believe that they are right. I know it breaks your heart every time you hear those insults, and they keep playing inside your head like a record, but please try to be kind to yourself. You have been through a lot, and so has your body. Let us now take a step toward healing and learn how to love ourselves better.

Tips for Improving Body Image

A negative body image is one of the leading reasons why we have so much hatred for our bodies. We have already talked about why one can develop a negative body image; now, let us discuss the ways to overcome a negative body image so that you can begin to love yourself a bit more.

Stop Fat-Shaming

There is a notion that perfect bodies are supposed to be thin without an ounce of fat on them. Media and the glamor industry are responsible for this kind of thought, and now, being beautiful is equated with being thin. If you want to build a positive body image, you must fight fatism and embrace people having bodies of all shapes and sizes. Think about a few people from your personal life whom you admire. Do all of them have the so-called perfect body? The answer will help you realize that a person's body size has nothing to do with their personality. Forming an opinion based on societal standards will take you nowhere because those standards keep changing every few years. In the 1950s, Marilyn Monroe was considered one of the most iconic beauties of the time. She was a full-bodied woman and wore size-14 dresses. Today, she'd probably be considered fat and not given a chance to act in any movies. So, societal trends make no sense, and you must form your opinion based on logic.

Diet for Good Health

Nowadays, there is a craze about following extreme diets in order to lose weight. People are following keto diets, intermittent fasting diets, and many other forms of diet so that they can have the perfect body. Celebrities and influencers also have a huge role in promoting these diets and advocating their benefits. A healthy and balanced diet is important for your health, but that does not mean you have to starve yourself every other day. Just because your favorite star is advocating intermittent fasting does not mean you have to do it too. Every person's body is different and so are their food requirements. A balanced diet is called "balanced" because it includes everything in the right proportions. Cutting down on carbohydrates and fats can have harmful effects on your body, especially if you are a teenager. If you really want to follow a diet, consult a nutritionist and get a plan that works for you. Do not shame yourself for craving a dessert or adding an extra slice of cheese to your sandwich. A healthy diet that fulfills all your physical requirements is essential when you are building a positive body image.

You Can't Change Your Genes

Positive body image building starts with learning to accept that certain things in your body cannot be changed. Although advancements in cosmetic surgery have made it possible to change certain body parts, they can have long-lasting side effects and are not recommended. Genetics play a significant role in determining your looks and physical features, which is why the wisest thing you can do is to accept them. Once you are okay with the fact that certain parts of your body are a result of your genes, self-acceptance becomes easier. In fact, you should embrace those features as a part of your heritage. Maybe your nose is a bit crooked like your grandfather's, but that means a part of him and his legacy is living through you. Be proud of your genetics and it will be easier to develop a positive attitude toward your body.

Figure Out Your Emotions Behind the Attitude

When you are calling yourself "fat" or "ugly," ask yourself if it's just about your body, or are there deeper issues inside your mind that are making you feel this way. Maybe you failed a test or could not accomplish something that you thought you would and that is making you angry at yourself. Instead of being angry about the event, you are directing your frustrations toward your body. Do not ignore your *real* feelings and remember not to cool off your anger by body-shaming yourself. In doing so, you are causing more damage than you can imagine.

Question the Messages on Media

Like I said earlier, brands only care about making money, so they are going to push unrealistic standards on customers so that the fear of missing out makes them try extreme measures to conform to those standards. Whenever you are shopping online, the model who is wearing the clothes is usually a tall woman wearing a small-sized dress. If you think about it logically, women who are tall are likely to have a slightly broader build and might not always wear a dress that is small-sized. This creates a misconception among people because their size is quite different. Media will always generalize problematic standards for their benefit, but it is your responsibility to rationalize the same.

There are debates regarding popular indices, like the Body Mass Index, which are used to measure whether a person is overweight or obese based on their height and weight. However, it does not consider factors like bone and muscle density, which determine the weight of a person. Somebody who has heavy bones or high muscle density may be overweight or even obese according to the Body Mass Index. Therefore, following anything blindly can cause you a lot of distress and you might start to see your body as something that it is not.

Learning to Love Your Body

People who have experienced body shaming are more likely to hate their bodies than others who haven't. However, most people suffer from varying degrees of body dissatisfaction, which contributes to their self-esteem issues. Loving your body when you have been shamed all your life can be a daunting task, but it is essential for your mental health. Here are a few ways that can make loving your body easier:

- Commit to the fact that you want to change your thought process. Once you acknowledge that you have a negative relationship with your body, it becomes easier to start the process. Remember, even after you start this process, there will be instances of body-shaming. You can feel sad after such encounters, but you cannot give up on developing this journey.

- Try to eliminate the conception that looking a certain way is going to solve all your problems. People who are victims of body shaming often feel that if they stopped looking the way they do now, the shaming would go away. However, that is not necessarily true because your shamer will find some other grounds to shame and insult you. A change in your appearance will not bring about happiness. The proof of that lies in the fact that many celebrities suffer from depression and addictions, despite looking flawless all the time. Moreover, if you feel that if you start looking a certain way then you will gain more love and respect from your close family and friends, then maybe it is time to review your social circle.

- Stop judging other people based on their appearance. Neither celebrities nor your friends deserve that kind of judgment. One of the most essential steps to learning to love your body is to adopt a more body-positive attitude toward the entire world. Every time you are judging someone based on their looks, you are reinforcing to yourself that it is okay to measure a person's value like that.

- Cleanse your social media from time to time. I know it is impractical to ask someone to stay off social media completely in order to avoid any triggers. Therefore, you should block or mute people or posts that might invoke feelings of shame inside you. Last year, I fractured my leg and was put on bed rest for a couple of months. Naturally, due to lack of movement, I was gaining weight and could not follow a properly balanced diet. It was also difficult to cook all that food with a broken leg. I spent a good part of that time on the bed scrolling through social media, and whenever I saw someone put up a workout video, I would panic and feel anxious because I was currently unable to even move properly. After a while, I decided to mute every post that gave me anxiety. It might seem stupid, but it works. Make sure that you follow pages and posts related to things that you love. For me, they are dogs, poetry, and artwork. Whatever works for you and makes you happy should fill your newsfeed. Staying away from negativity will do wonders when you are on a journey to love your body.

- Get to know your body properly. Try out various forms of exercise that require body control, like yoga, belly dancing, or weightlifting. It is important to note that none of these activities are gender-specific and can therefore be practiced by everyone. You can also perform an effective mindfulness exercise known as a body scan. Close your eyes, and after a few deep breaths, focus entirely on your body. Start from your feet and slowly move up to your head. Focus carefully on each part and try to understand whether you feel pain or any other sensation. Concentrate on what your body is trying to tell you; you will be amazed by how much you can learn. Physically touching various parts of your body can also be an eye-opening experience. I know it may sound a bit creepy, but the more you get to know your body, the more you will be able to love it.

- Try to make your body feel like it is appreciated and respected. It does not always have to be something very fancy. In fact, you can do all kinds of stupid things if it makes you feel good. You can put on a face mask and listen to your favorite jazz music, or you can put on those fuzzy pairs of socks that make your feet feel warm. This exercise is effective because it makes your body feel good and lifts your spirits. It's like giving yourself a hug and giving your body a reminder that you appreciate everything it's doing for you.

- Use positive affirmations to build a more positive body image. Many people might find it stupid, but positive affirmations do wonders to boost your self-esteem. When you repeat positive things repeatedly, your brain starts to believe that they are true. The same thing is true for negative things as well, which is what leads people to shame themselves. Replace the negative thoughts about your body with positive affirmations and see the change. Write down positive words like, "I love my body and I respect it," "I am perfect and so is my body," or, "I am awesome for taking such good care of myself." Write the affirmations in your journal and read them out every morning after waking up and before going to bed. You can also read them out if you are feeling depressed and need an ego boost. There is another practice that I have found useful for my bad days. I write down one thing I like about myself on a piece of paper every day for a couple of months, then I place that piece of paper inside a jar. You can do it too, then stop when the jar is full. On those days when you are feeling particularly bad about yourself, you can open the jar and pick up a piece of paper. You will find something that you like about yourself, which will make you feel better.

- Meditate often to feel good about your body. Meditation is a good way to get to know yourself and bring clarity to your thoughts. To start, try some of the simple guided-meditation techniques and then gradually move to an advanced level as your concentration improves. The reason why meditation works is because it guides you to stay in the moment and not drift away in spiralling thoughts. This has a cleansing effect on your subconscious mind and lets you appreciate your body more. Mediation is a scientifically proven way to reduce stress, anxiety, and a variety of other issues. Initially, you might have trouble concentrating and your mind will wander, but once you get into the habit of it, you will feel the benefits.

- You can try neuro-linguistic programming techniques to apply the methods used by successful people and replicate them to achieve your personal goals. The techniques will help you to identify the underlying causes of body image issues and take appropriate action in order to get out of them. Neuro-linguistic programming encourages the formation of positive thought patterns, which help people to develop a healthier relationship with their body.

- See a professional therapist. Although there is still a lot of stigma around consulting a psychologist, as an educated and aware person, you should appreciate the need for therapy. Despite knowing all the methods, one might still have a hard time in getting over the negative body image that they have created for themselves. When you see a therapist, they can help you to navigate your thoughts in the direction of self-compassion. It can become a safe space to vent about the most trivial issues and your therapist will listen to you without any judgment because that is their job. Once you start therapy, you will discover a lot of issues and problems hidden inside your mind, and that realization is going to solve a lot of riddles. I speak from personal experience that therapy can be eye-opening. Your body image issues are linked with several other behavioral patterns and coping mechanisms, and therapy helps you identify them and work through them. Of course, it is not magic, so it will take a lot of time. At the beginning, you might even feel that you are not making any progress but be patient. Follow the instructions and exercises that your therapist gives you and believe in yourself that you will be able to make a change. You need to let the therapist help you because it is a two-way process. Unless you are willing to help yourself, it is unlikely that someone else will be able to help you.

Imagine it is the middle of the night and you are having a breakdown. You are crying on your bathroom floor and you feel like there cannot be anything worse than this. Almost all of us have had nights like these when everything seems pathetic and like you have lost the will to carry on. In those moments, all advice about mental health and positivity fail to reach you. But do you give up? No. Because your brain knows that this is temporary, and that you will soon get over it. Your body tries its best to hold you through those tough hours.

No matter how many friends you have, in your darkest moments, it is *you* who always picks *you* up. You cry, complain, scream your lungs out, or sob in silence. But you always get up, and your body caresses you as you recover from it. Your body takes such good care of you all the time, so it is only fair that you do the same to it. Think of your body as your best friend—never insult it. The image you see in the mirror is the person who holds you together and supports you in everything you do. It might be a size smaller or larger than what you want it to be, but it is doing it's very best. Stand up to your shamer, but never shame yourself. You deserve nothing but love and respect. Believe it, and good things will come your way. The tunnel is not as dark as your mind imagines it to be, and the light is not as far away as you think. Embrace your darkness, and you will find the light within you.

Conclusion:
You Are A Winner in This Battle

My mother was interested in beauty and skincare. She visited the salon every month for grooming and hairstyling because she always wanted to look perfect. One evening when I was in middle school after my mother came back from the salon, I saw that she was unusually quiet and sad. I asked her if she was okay. She did not say much but I knew something was up. Later, when my dad came home, I overheard my mom crying to him, telling him how a lady who worked at the parlor had told her she should not wear sleeveless dresses because her body was not shapely. My dad tried to console her, but she kept crying, and I felt very sad. My sister was then around four or five months old, which meant my mom was still recovering from the delivery. Postpartum bodies often look different—and that is fine—because they have gone through so much. Even after all these years, I still remember her crying because, when somebody goes through body shaming, the people close to them are also affected by it.

It is not uncommon for beauticians and ladies working at parlors to shame their customers into buying a new product. In fact, many advertisements still focus on shaming their prospective customers in order to promote their products. The world has become an ugly place and it is pathetic how low brands can stoop to earn the extra bucks. However, despite the negativity, there are many celebrities and people who are spreading the messages of body positivity. I know it is easy to say, but you should try to focus on the good because you deserve everything good in the world. You have survived body shaming, and you have emerged a winner.

It is not easy when someone criticizes you and makes you feel small, but always remember that your worth is not calculated by other people's opinions. Don't be harsh on yourself just because some stupid person thought it was okay to shame you. It is not your fault. You are beautiful and perfect just the way you are. Body shamers insult other people because of some hidden insecurities within themselves. I know it is difficult to feel anything but hatred for the person insulting you but try to pity them because they are so mean and small that their only source of pleasure comes from picking on other people's insecurities. Mostly, it has nothing to do with you; they simply want to express their power over you, so that they can make you feel small. But you cannot let those words get to you, which is why it is extremely important that you be kind to yourself.

Even after all the instructions and having a ready response, if you were unable to stand up for yourself, and suffered in silence when someone was body shaming you, do not blame yourself. You tried your best! It often becomes difficult to act at the right time because our brain is so overcome with feelings and emotions. Therefore, many times after an argument is over, we remember the things that we were *supposed* to say. You are a human being, and you can feel overwhelmed when something like this happens. When you have been shamed, you go through mental turmoil. Don't add to that distress by indulging in negative self-talk. Your body needs your love and support, not further humiliation. Do whatever makes you feel good. Take a walk, order some good food, do some journaling, or simply cry and let it all out. The more you hold on to the negative thoughts, the more aggravated they become.

Due to the intensity of body shaming, you sometimes start believing that maybe the shamer was right. Maybe you *are* ugly and pathetic. If something like this happens, try to picture yourself as a young child. You can even paste a picture of yourself as a child on your table. Look at the kid, and ask yourself, *how would you treat them?* If someone told this child they were ugly, would you encourage them? Or would you knock that person down, trying to protect the child? I guess you know the answer. There is still that child inside you and you must do everything in your power to protect them. Whenever you feel hatred for your body, think of the child. Would you let them hate their body? What would you tell them if they came up to you and said that they find themselves ugly? Give yourself the same kind of reassurance that you would give a child. That is how you should treat yourself.

Getting over body-shaming is extremely difficult, whether it happens physically or online. You cannot control what other people are saying, but you *can* stand up to them and make them understand that you do not approve of their behavior. Loving yourself is a process, and it will not happen overnight. You must be gentle and patient with yourself.

Now that you have finished this book, you are one step closer to becoming a strong and independent person who knows their true self-worth. Always remember that it all begins with your will to stand up and put a stop to any kind of insulting behavior. You are already halfway there because you chose to read this book, and therefore, to heal yourself. Now it is time to step out bravely, sporting any look that you like, without worrying about what people are going to say. Don't be scared to be bold and challenge societal norms because you don't need to round your edges in order to fit in. Good luck!

References

Assistant Secretary for Public Affairs (ASPA). (2019,
     September 24). *What Is Cyberbullying.*
     StopBullying.gov.
     https://www.stopbullying.gov/cyberbullying/what-is-
     it

Body Image – Get Help for Body Image Issues. (n.d.).
     Www.goodtherapy.org.
     https://www.goodtherapy.org/learn-about-
     therapy/issues/body-image/get-help

*Body Image issues and negative body image help in
     Edinburgh.* (n.d.). Nlptherapyedinburgh.co.uk.
     Retrieved September 27, 2021, from
     https://nlptherapyedinburgh.co.uk/how-nlp-can-
     help-you/body-image/

Body image: What is it, and how can I improve it? (2020,
     September 16). Www.medicalnewstoday.com.
     https://www.medicalnewstoday.com/articles/249190
     #considerations-for-lgbtqia-communities

Body Shaming. What It Is & How To Overcome It | ANAD.
     (n.d.). National Association of Anorexia Nervosa and
     Associated Disorders. https://anad.org/get-
     informed/body-image/body-image-articles/body-
     shaming/

Brazier, Y. (2020, October 11). *Body image: What is it and how can I improve it?* Www.medicalnewstoday.com. https://www.medicalnewstoday.com/articles/249190

Capadose, O. (2019, May 17). *How to Handle Body Shaming*. The Mix. https://www.themix.org.uk/mental-health/body-image-and-self-esteem/how-to-handle-body-shaming-32324.html

Clarity Clinic. (2020, April 30). *Body Shaming: Its Affect on Young & Old*. Clarity Clinic. https://www.claritychi.com/body-shaming-in-elderly/

DEVLIN, K. (2019). *NPR Choice page*. Npr.org. https://www.npr.org/templates/story/story.php?storyId=106268439

Fat shame others. (2019, May 18). The Times of India. https://timesofindia.indiatimes.com/life-style/health-fitness/health-news/7-ways-you-might-be-accidentally-body-shaming-your-friend/photostory/69386286.cms?picid=69386287

Gonsalves, K. (2015, March 11). *10 Things To Stop Doing If You Want To Love Your Body*. Mindbodygreen. https://www.mindbodygreen.com/0-17640/10-things-to-stop-doing-if-you-want-to-love-your-body.html

Hartung, E. (2018). *The 10 Warning Signs of Cyberbullying*. Netnanny.com. https://www.netnanny.com/blog/the-10-warning-signs-of-cyberbullying/

Hawkins, N. (2009, November 18). *Negative Body Image - Understanding and Overcoming*. Center for Change. https://centerforchange.com/battling-bodies-understanding-overcoming-negative-body-images/?__cf_chl_managed_tk__=pmd_ronz2.hDe aBkt0PVHdTz7rjEHw1mRvv7mhnT3007eww-1632377390-0-gqNtZGzNA5CjcnBszQmR

Leigh Smith, D. (2020, August 25). *10 Surprising Ways to Improve Your Body Image—No Dieting Required*. The Healthy. https://www.thehealthy.com/mental-health/body-positivity/improve-body-image/

Lickteig, B. (n.d.). *Social Media: Cyberbullying, Body Shaming, and Trauma – The Child Advocacy Center of Lapeer County*. Caclapeer.org. https://caclapeer.org/social-media-cyberbullying-body-shaming-and-trauma/

Mayo Clinic. (2016). *Body dysmorphic disorder - Symptoms and causes*. Mayo Clinic. https://www.mayoclinic.org/diseases-conditions/body-dysmorphic-disorder/symptoms-causes/syc-20353938

Mayo Clinic. (2018, February 20). *Anorexia Nervosa - Symptoms and causes*. Mayo Clinic; Mayo Clinic.

https://www.mayoclinic.org/diseases-
conditions/anorexia-nervosa/symptoms-causes/syc-
20353591

Mayo Clinic Staff. (2018, May 10). *Bulimia nervosa -
Symptoms and causes*. Mayo Clinic.
https://www.mayoclinic.org/diseases-
conditions/bulimia/symptoms-causes/syc-20353615

National Eating Disorders Collaboration. (n.d.). *Body
Image*. Nedc.com.au. https://nedc.com.au/eating-
disorders/eating-disorders-explained/body-image/

Neuro–Linguistic Programming. (2013). Goodtherapy.org.
https://www.goodtherapy.org/learn-about-
therapy/types/neuro-linguistic-programming

Patchin, J. W. (2018, July 23). *Standing up to
Cyberbullying: Top Ten Tips for Teens*. Cyberbullying
Research Center. https://cyberbullying.org/standing-
up-to-cyberbullying-tips-for-teens

Richards, A. (2015, November 10). *7 Things To Remember
When Confronted With Body Shaming*. Bustle.
https://www.bustle.com/articles/121288-7-things-to-
remember-when-confronted-with-body-shaming

SAHA, A. (2020, September 11). *What Is Body Shaming And
Its Effects On Mental Health?* Www.psychologs.com.
https://www.psychologs.com/article/what-is-body-
shaming-and-its-effects-on-mental-health

Securly. (2018, October 4). *The 10 Types of Cyberbullying.*
Securly Blog; Securly Blog.
https://blog.securly.com/2018/10/04/the-10-types-
of-cyberbullying/

Stand Up to Cyberbullying. (2012, November 1).
#RGSTeachersLounge.
https://blog.reallygoodstuff.com/stand-up-
cyberbullying-stops-now/

Thisiseloise, E. @. (2020, November 20). *Body shamers:
How to stand up to them.* Heart Your Body.
https://heartyourbody.co.uk/stand-up-to-body-
shamers/

UNICEF. (2020). *Cyberbullying: What is it and how to stop
it.* Www.unicef.org; UNICEF.
https://www.unicef.org/end-violence/how-to-stop-
cyberbullying

Vargas, E. (2013, December 4). *Body Shaming: What Is It &
Why Do We Do It?* Walden Eating Disorders; Walden
Eating Disorders.
https://www.waldeneatingdisorders.com/blog/body-
shaming-what-is-it-why-do-we-do-it/

What are the effects of cyberbullying? (2021, June 10).
Www.kaspersky.com.
https://www.kaspersky.com/resource-
center/preemptive-safety/cyberbullying-effects